# Contents

Foreword                                                                v

1. **A brief history of mental health services**                        **1**
   How a mental health agenda emerged                                   1
   Tightening the rules                                                 3
   Towards a National Health Service                                    5
   The shift into the community                                         6
   Plugging the gaps                                                    8

2. **Demand for mental health services**                                **11**
   The scale of the problem                                            11
   Main mental health problems in the UK                               11
   Access to services                                                  14

3. **The structure of mental health services**                          **17**
   Who commissions care?                                               17
   Who provides care?                                                  18
   Structures to oversee quality                                       23

4. **How mental health services are delivered**                         **27**
   Primary care                                                        27
   Community care                                                      28
   Integrating the care programme approach                            29
   Acute and specialist care                                          30
   How many people are admitted?                                      30

Guardianship                                      31

Mental health staff                               31


5.  **Government policy on mental health**        **37**

    The national service framework                37

    Scotland, Wales and Northern Ireland          42

    The NHS plan                                  42

    Scotland's plan                               44

    Compulsory treatment outside hospitals        45


6.  **Controversies in mental health services**   **47**

    The funding debate                            47

    Workforce issues                              49

    Structural change                             52

    Legal reform                                  53

    Reform of secure services                     54

    Cultural attitudes                            54


7.  **The future of mental health services**      **57**


**Further reading**                               **59**


**Glossary**                                      **60**

# Foreword

Few areas of healthcare are so prone to controversy as mental health. Time and again mental health services and their users find themselves the stuff of lurid, sensationalist press headlines. Deep-seated fears about mental illness fuel popular prejudice, and all too often surround mentally ill people with hysteria and stigma. Controversy flourishes within mental health services, too – about, for example, the availability of the latest treatments, how to deal with those suffering dangerous severe personality disorders or whether the level of funding is adequate. Throughout the NHS's history, mental health has been perceived as the poor relation alongside primary care or general acute services.

While caring for most mentally ill people in the community has long been recognised as a far better option than confining them in Victorian long-stay asylums, implementing the policy has been painfully slow with many mistakes along the way and a sense that resources for mental health services have been short-changed in the process. The policy has attracted a lot of public suspicion, so much so that even within the last couple of years – and despite the obvious improvements in quality of life it has brought for mentally ill people – publicity-conscious ministers in unguarded moments expressed the view that care in the community had been a failure. Nevertheless, they have persevered with it, and emphasis now is on making it work – partly by allaying public fears about safety, partly by instigating a panoply of quality-control measures. Like every other part of the health service, mental healthcare is currently subject to the government's modernisation programme, laid out in the NHS plan. Major change is on the way, including revisions to mental health legislation and how the NHS works with local authorities to provide services.

This short guide aims to put mental health services in their historical context and explain older, more familiar terms as well as new ones. We hope, therefore, that readers will feel it is a useful means of finding their bearings in a fast-moving area.

Peter Davies, Editor, Health Service Journal, May 2001.

# 1. A brief history of mental health services

Until the mid-18th century, people recognised as 'insane' had no legal protection. Over the next 100 years asylums and lunatic institutions were brought under national jurisdiction – but more as a means to protect the public than sympathy for the plight of those locked away. During the latter half of the 20th century mental healthcare, now under the auspices of the NHS, was brought out of the asylums and into the community. This persisted until 1998, when the Labour government declared community care a failure, outlining new ways of working in its national service framework for mental health.

## How a mental health agenda emerged

The concept of there being a group of people who need special protection because of problems with their mental health first emerged in the UK in the mid-18th century.

At this time, there was no such thing as a medical profession and certainly no network of social care. Anyone recognised as insane had no protection in law. The Poor Law, which allowed parishes to provide for relief of their own paupers by means of taxation, failed to distinguish between the 'impotent poor' who could not work, and the able-bodied poor, who would not.

Conditions varied massively from parish to parish, and there was no universal system of classification. In many areas, the task of administering help to the 'impotent' simply fell by the wayside and they ended up in workhouses or prisons, where conditions were, more often than not, appalling.

Mentally ill people living near London might be sent to 'Bedlam', the only public institution dealing with the 'mentally abnormal'. If they were from a wealthy background, their relatives might send them to a small, private 'madhouse', which charged high fees in return for keeping their inmates absolutely secret.

## A brief history of Bedlam

Bedlam, real name Bethlem, took its name from a priory of the Order of St Mary of Bethlehem founded in London in 1247. It was seized by the Crown in 1375 and used as an institution for the reception of those suffering from acute mental disorder from

*William Hogarth,* A Rake's Progress, *published 1735 – the final scene, shown here, is set in Bethlem Hospital.*

1377 onwards. In 1547 Henry VIII granted the hospital to the City of London, and 10 years later the management was transferred to the governors of the original Bridewell prison at Blackfriars.

This arrangement continued until the Bethlem - now the Royal Bethlem and on its fourth site, in Beckenham, Kent - joined with the Maudsley Hospital to form the Institute of Psychiatry, the only postgraduate teaching hospital exclusive to psychiatry. It became part of the NHS in 1948.

The Maudsley, for its part, had been founded in 1915 thanks to a donation from Dr Henry Maudsley, a pioneering psychiatrist. Its aim was to deal exclusively with early and acute cases; to operate an outpatients clinic; and to provide for teaching and research on the diagnosis and treatment of mental disorder. The two hospitals are now part of the South London and Maudsley NHS trust.

Three separate sets of events during the 18th century led imperceptibly to reform in the way mentally ill people were treated.

The first was the inclusion of the category 'dangerous lunatics' in a revision of the vagrancy laws in 1744; for the first time legislation stipulated that parishes should pay for the 'keeping, maintaining and curing' of such individuals. The second was a period of public alarm during the 1760s and early 1770s about revelations concerning conditions in private madhouses. The third was the development of a less condemnatory attitude towards madness, brought about by George III's famed illness, details of which emerged from 1789 onwards.

During the second half of the century, three lunatic institutions sprang up voluntarily in major cities – St Luke's Hospital in London, the Manchester Lunatic Hospital and the York Retreat. County asylums followed in the early years of the 19th century.

Following a select committee inquiry into the appalling conditions in asylums and workhouses in 1815-16, reformers attempted to introduce several parliamentary bills with a view to establishing an inspectorate – but these failed after opposition from the Lords.

By 1828, there were nine county asylums in operation. The County Asylums Act of the same year provided for visiting justices to visit asylums and send annual returns of admissions, discharges and deaths to the home secretary. The Madhouse Act covered all private madhouses and subscription hospitals (except Bethlem); it also brought the power of inspection into the hands of commissioners appointed by the state.

From 1842-5 these commissioners, led by Lord Ashley, conducted a tour of inspection, leading to the hugely significant Lunacy Report and the Lunatics Act of 1845. This created a full-time inspectorate covering all hospitals and licensed houses in the country, including Bethlem; inspectors even had the power to visit single lunatics. They could also visit prisons and workhouses.

## Tightening the rules

Legal reform continued through the second half of the 19th century – although it was normally borne out of fear that poor conditions would, if unchecked, make the insane more dangerous, rather than out of sympathy with their plight.

An 1862 act tightened the procedures relating to private certification of lunatics, making clear that the first certificate should be valid for only three months; the order confining the patient should be sent to the commissioners within 24 hours, and they should visit the patient 'as soon as possible'.

In 1874 a new four shillings per head grant-in-aid for each pauper lunatic placed in an asylum gave an incentive for boards of guardians to remove mentally ill paupers from the workhouse to an asylum – where curative treatment might at least stand a chance of being offered.

After many years of parliamentary conflict over the subject, the Lunacy Act of 1890 set down in great detail the future of mental health services. It retained the lunacy commissioners, appointed by the lord chancellor. It brought public asylums into the jurisdiction of county or borough councils, each of which was compelled for the first time to build and maintain an asylum. The local authority would appoint visiting committees.

Under the new legislation, there were three main ways one could be admitted to an asylum. The first, admittance by reception order, involved a relative stating their connection with the patient and making a

*A patient suffering from 'acute mania' at Bethlem Royal Hospital, 1850s.*

*The same patient, convalescent at Bethlem Royal Hospital, 1850s.*

statement before a justice of the peace, supported by two medical certificates. Admittance by urgency order was used when there was no time for a reception order, and the procedure involved just a relative's petition and one medical certificate. Admittance by summary reception order was the most common method of admission for pauper patients. Details were also set down about a range of issues, including visitation frequencies, keeping of medical records, appeals by patients and discharge procedures.

In the meantime, public debate heated up around the issue of 'mental defectives' or the 'feeble-minded', as distinct from the insane or lunatic. The 1899 Elementary Education

(Defective and Epileptic Children) Act empowered all education authorities to set up special schools or classes for 'feeble-minded' children of school age, or to board them out to a suitable school if necessary.

A Royal Commission on the care of the feeble-minded from 1904-8 came to the conclusion that heredity was an important factor in mental deficiency. In addition, other social problems – especially delinquency, alcoholism and illegitimacy – were aggravated by the fact that so many defectives were allowed freedom of action in the community. But contrary to the views of the growing eugenics movement, the commission insisted that the main criterion in certification must be the protection and happiness of the defective themselves, rather than the purification of the race.

Five years later, the 1913 Mental Deficiency Act set out, for the first time, definitions of different classes of mental defective: idiots, imbeciles, feeble-minded persons and moral defectives. It clarified the certification process for these various individuals; set up a board of control to supervise county and local-level provision; and made local authorities each set up mental deficiency committees, composed mainly of council members, but also including co-opted members – some of them women. For the first time, mental deficiency was to be dealt with primarily in social terms: regardless of its cause, the ultimate test was to be social incapacity. And, in the same year, a new education act made the 1899 act's provisions compulsory rather than merely permissible.

The Mental Deficiency Act of 1927 widened the definition of mental defectiveness to any 'condition of arrested or incomplete development of mind existing before the age of 18, whether arising from inherent causes or induced by disease or injury'. In doing so, the emphasis shifted from segregation at all costs to a variety of provisions which were suited to the needs of the individual.

## Towards a National Health Service

During the 1920s and 1930s the treatment of neurosis developed in leaps and bounds, but away from the asylums, which were largely custodial in function. London's highly influential Tavistock Clinic, a multidisciplinary psychodynamic centre, opened in 1920, for example, and the Maudsley Hospital opened to voluntary patients in 1923 (see *A brief history of Bedlam,* page 2).

Standards in the asylums, increasingly known as mental hospitals, were extremely poor; but policy-makers were at least now making the right noises about the extension of voluntary treatment and higher professional standards in psychiatry, outpatient clinics and aftercare work.

In 1920 the new Ministry of Health took over powers in the control of lunacy and mental deficiency. The 1930 Mental Treatment Act reorganised the board of control, made provisions for voluntary treatment, gave official blessing to the establishment of psychiatric outpatient clinics, and abolished outmoded terminology such as 'lunatic', which now became 'patient' or 'person of unsound mind', depending on the context.

Mental health training for a wide range of professionals, including doctors, nurses and social workers, developed during this period. A greater sense of direction emerged through both Dame Ellen Pinsent's ground-breaking 1937 review of mental health services in Oxfordshire and the Feversham Report on voluntary services in 1939.

After the war, mental health services came under the wing of plans to create the new National Health Service, with psychiatry largely being treated like any other branch of medicine, and mental hospitals therefore coming under the authority of the new regional hospital boards. Local authorities were charged with the 'prevention, care and aftercare of illness and mental defectiveness'. The minister for health became the central authority for mental health; the advisory central health services council was to include two doctors and two laymen (out of a total of 41) with knowledge and experience of mental health services.

Some of the legislation creating the NHS was open-ended, allowing for a great variation in practice between areas. This meant that provision of services could be patchy. Some areas created new mental health schemes providing comprehensive care; others did the bare minimum. Some communicated well with hospital services; others remained more isolated.

### The 1959 Mental Health Act

- The act gave definitions of mental disorder; arrested or incomplete development of mind (broken down into subnormality and severe subnormality), and psychopathic disorder.
- It dissolved the board of control, provided greater clarity on what services local authorities should be providing, and gave mental welfare officers powers of entry and inspection. New mental health review tribunals were to take over the board of control's watchdog functions.
- Most patients would now be admitted to hospital voluntarily. Those entering compulsorily could be admitted according to tight rules relating to either an observation order, a treatment order (both recommended by two doctors) or an emergency order (three days maximum and backed by one doctor).
- Other rules were laid down about care and treatment in hospital, discharge, guardianship and patients concerned in criminal proceedings.

## The shift into the community

During the 1950s, enormous changes occurred. This was thanks to three 'revolutions' – the development of tranquillisers; mental hospitals' 'open-door' movement bringing their work closer to that of the community services; and a movement for legal reform, culminating in the 1959 Mental Health Act.

The 'open-door' movement was a policy pursued by mental hospitals increasingly during the 1950s. They acknowledged that the hospitals were just one among a whole raft of tools at the disposal of the medico-social team – the others included outpatient, day and domiciliary care. The effect was a dramatic drop in the length of stay of short-stay patients. But in parallel, there was a rise in admissions – especially re-admissions – which led some observers to comment that the open door was really a revolving one.

The 'open-door' policy was a result of shifting opinion among professionals, the new opportunities thrown up by psychotropic drugs and 'official' inputs such as the report of the World Health Organisation's Third Expert Committee on Mental Health in 1953 and the Royal Commission on the Law Relating to Mental Illness and Mental Deficiency, which eventually led to the 1959 act (see box, page 6).

The act marked the turning point, after which mental health services began to officially shift towards being community-based. Enoch Powell famously declared war on the mental hospitals in 1961, describing them as 'the defences we have to storm' and even declaring that the government would rather see them derelict than put to new use.

A year later Powell produced a 10-year plan setting out the community services which local authorities should, in theory, provide as a replacement for the asylums. But the economy was faltering through much of the 1960s and 1970s, meaning the money to match the rhetoric did not appear. Bed numbers certainly fell during this period, but this often just meant that remaining patients were treated at a higher unit cost. Little money leaked over the health/local government divide to support former hospital residents. The first asylum did not, in fact, close until 1986.

From 1972 local authority social services departments were created, providing the full range of personal social services. Later in the decade, some limited attempts were made to shift money from NHS into local authority funding streams.

The 1975 White Paper *Better services for the mentally ill* examined the development of services – or lack of it – since the 1962 hospital plan. It set out a blueprint for integrated mental healthcare involving health, social and voluntary-sector inputs.

Especially given that it appeared during a time of severe recession, it did little to improve the haphazard dissolution of the hospitals, nor to enable statutory authorities to provide adequate community-based care.

The 1983 Mental Health Act provided safeguards for people in hospital, and imposed a duty on district health authorities and social services departments to provide after-care services for people discharged from hospital, in co-operation with voluntary agencies.

## Plugging the gaps

A 1985 select committee report stated that hospital closures had outrun community care provision, especially in relation to mental health patients. It called for government action and increased spending. A year later, an Audit Commission report found that despite the drop in hospital beds, local authorities had not been allocated the resources necessary to provide alternative forms of care.

In 1988 a report on mental health services by Sir Roy Griffiths recommended the transfer of all community care to local authorities, with 'earmarked' grants from central government and local authorities able to purchase services from other agencies.

The 1989 *Caring for people* white paper, based on the Griffiths report, set out the framework for changes to community care, including a new purchaser/provider funding structure for social care. It promoted the development of domiciliary, daycare and respite services to enable people to live independently in their own homes. Such services did, indeed, mushroom throughout the 1990s, with local authorities responsible for assessing need, designing care packages and ensuring their delivery.

The care programme approach, introduced in 1991, set out a framework for HAs, laying down how they should ensure people with mental health problems received appropriate levels of support in the community. This would rely on liaison between them and social care agencies.

Under the new regime, local authorities were expected to publish community care plans outlining plans for the development of community-based services. They were also responsible for registering and inspecting homes and other community services purchased or provided by themselves. At the same time, however, HAs retained responsibility for providing long-term healthcare for those in need.

In 1993 guidance, the government created a supervision register, on which could be placed people who were considered to be 'at risk of harming themselves or other people'. The aim of it was to ensure they remained in contact with mental health services and had their care monitored regularly.

The 1994 framework for local community care charters stated that social services departments should draw up local charters in collaboration with HAs and housing departments, giving people clear information about what they could expect from local authorities and criteria against which they could measure and improve their services.

A 1996 act bestowed new powers over after-care of people discharged from hospital. Another act placed a duty on local authorities to assess the needs of carers for services such as respite care.

In 1998, the new Labour government declared community care a failure. A year later it published its national service framework for mental health. It also published a consultation paper – jointly produced by the Home Office and Department of Health – entitled *Managing dangerous people with severe personality disorder*. This would introduce a new power of 'indeterminate but reviewable detention of dangerous personality-disordered individuals' who present a grave risk to the public'; as well as proposals for reforming the Mental Health Act.

# 2. Demand for mental health services

Around 30 per cent of people experience mental health problems in any given year. Two-thirds see their GP and just over 10 per cent of them are referred to a psychiatric service. People with schizophrenia are most likely to need hospital care. More people with mental illness are found in cities, though many people in rural areas may go undetected.

## The scale of the problem

Leading mental health charity Mind estimates that 300 out of every 1,000 adults in Great Britain experience mental health problems in any given year. Of these, 230 will visit a GP. Of these, 102 will be diagnosed as having a mental health problem. Of these, 24 will be referred to some kind of specialist psychiatric service. Of these, a handful will become an inpatient in some kind of psychiatric hospital. There are a total of around 4,000 suicides every year.

The box on page 12, overleaf, shows how many people with mental illness walk through the doors of specialist psychiatric services in the NHS per year, and how many are admitted to NHS facilities by age group.

## Main mental health problems in the UK

Mind quotes figures from the Office for National Statistics and other studies to suggest that the following are the main mental health problems experienced in Britain:

### Anxiety

The ONS estimates that 3.1 per cent of adults experience generalised anxiety disorders not including depression, at any given time. This estimate is in line with other studies showing a prevalence of between 2 and 5 per cent of the population. The ONS study shows that a further 7.7 per cent have mixed anxiety and depression, and that anxiety is far more common in women than in men – the prevalence among women is 9.9 per cent compared to 5.4 per cent in men.

Panic disorders, which are related to anxiety, appear in eight people per 1,000. This proportion is the same across all age groups and prevalence is approximately the same for both sexes.

## Depression

Depression with anxiety is experienced by 7.7 per cent of people in Great Britain, and depression without anxiety by 2.1 per cent. Overall, depression appears to occur in 10 per cent of the population at any given time. Estimates of lifetime prevalence vary from one in six to one in four. One in 20 people at any given time suffer from major or 'clinical' depression.

Women have a much higher prevalence of depression than men – it affects around 12 per cent of women compared to 7 per cent of men. Though some studies suggest depression occurs as often in men, women are twice as likely to be diagnosed and treated. The suggestion is that men tend to express their symptoms differently, for example through the use of alcohol and drugs, and are less likely to admit to the symptoms of depression.

### Annual NHS activity involving patients with mental illness

| Type of activity | Numbers |
| --- | --- |
| Finished consultant episode | 231,000 |
| Outpatient first attendance | 290,000 |
| Ward attendance | 93,000 |

*First contact with:*

| | |
| --- | --- |
| Clinical psychology services | 257,000 |
| Community psychiatric nursing | 584,000 |

*First attendance at NHS day care facility:*

| | |
| --- | --- |
| Mental illness | 62,000 |
| Old age psychiatry | 32,000 |
| Child and adolescent psychiatry | 2,000 |

| Admissions | Rate per 1,000 population |
| --- | --- |
| All ages | 4.3 |
| Under 15 | 0.1 |
| 15-19 | 2.1 |
| 20-24 | 5.0 |
| 25-44 | 5.5 |
| 45-64 | 3.7 |
| 65-74 | 5.3 |
| 75-84 | 11.3 |
| 85+ | 15.6 |

*Source: Department of Health.*
Figures are for England, 1997-98.

## Eating problems

The Mental Health Foundation estimates that up to 1 per cent of women in the UK between aged 15-30 have anorexia nervosa, and

*Up to 1 per cent of women in the UK aged 15-30 may have anorexia nervosa, which is more common in women than men.*

between 1 and 2 per cent bulimia nervosa. Many cases of eating disorders are unreported or undiagnosed, however, so the actual figures are likely to be much higher. Eating disorders are much more likely to occur among women than men, although there is evidence to suggest that up to 25 per cent of anorexia cases in the younger age group (7-14) are boys.

### Postnatal depression

The most common form of postnatal disturbance is called the 'baby blues', said to be experienced by more than half of all mothers in the western world. The baby blues generally last 12-24 hours and occur between the third and sixth day after the birth.

But at least 10 per cent of new mothers experience full postnatal depression, which can occur at any time in the baby's first year of life, although different studies claim prevalence levels of 3-22 per cent. Around half of all cases will never come to medical attention, however. Puerperal psychosis – a severe and relatively rare form of postnatal depression – affects around one new mother in 500.

### Dementia

A fifth of people in the UK over the age of 80, and 6 per cent over the age of 65, are affected by dementia.

Around 650,000 people with dementia are known to UK health authorities. More than two-thirds of these are diagnosed with Alzheimer's disease. The Mental Health Foundation estimates that Alzheimer's

John Robertson

*A nurse talks to a younger patient with Alzheimer's disease – thought to affect one in 1,000 under-65s.*

disease affects 1 in 1,000 people under 65; 3 per cent of people over 65 and 10-15 per cent of people over 80.

## Phobias

The ONS estimates that just over 1 per cent of British adults experience phobias. Women are twice as likely as men to experience phobias. Two studies suggest major underreporting of phobias – one in Canada gave a prevalence of 7.7 per cent and one in the US, 13.3 per cent.

## Personality disorders

According to different studies, personality disorders affect from 2-13 per cent of people in Britain. The whole concept of personality disorder is controversial, so use of this diagnosis can often be questioned.

## Manic depression

Most studies give a lifetime prevalence of 1 per cent for manic depression (otherwise known as bipolar disorder), and equal rates for men and women. Hospital admission rates are higher because of the recurrent nature of the illness, although a fifth of people who have a first episode of manic depression do not get another.

## Obsessive compulsive disorder

Around 1.2 per cent of Britons have OCD at any given time, according to the ONS. Other studies suggest that up to 3 per cent of the population will experience the condition at some point during their lives. The ONS survey gives a female-to-male ratio of 15:9 for the disorder.

## Schizophrenia

Most studies show a lifetime prevalence of just under 1 per cent for schizophrenia, and prevalence rates of between two and four people per 1,000 at any given time. Prevalence rates are the same for men and women, but age and gender combined is an important factor – for example, incidence among men aged 15-24 is twice that for women.

## Access to services

People with schizophrenia are the group of patients most likely to need access to a hospital bed or other supported place during their illness. In 1992, for example, one in seven people with schizophrenia needed admission.

Mind claims that in terms of bed days, there are more NHS hospital inpatients with a diagnosis of schizophrenia than any other illness, either mental or physical. The charity estimates half of patients with schizophrenia have lost touch with NHS services; just over 10 per cent have their treatment managed by a GP, and 20 per cent have access to a community mental health nurse.

Rates of mental illness are higher in urban than in semi-rural or rural areas, reflecting the fact that people with severe mental health problems have a tendency to move into cities, and that being born in a city is also associated with a higher risk of developing schizophrenia. People in inner cities are more likely to live alone. Morbidity can also be more hidden in rural areas, because people living in smaller communities may be reluctant to seek help if they feel their anonymity could be compromised.

Access to services depends on a number of factors, including ethnic group, gender, social class, level of education and geographical location. There are a high number of compulsory admissions and admissions to secure beds from the African-Caribbean population.

A one-day census carried out on all psychiatric inpatients in acute and low-secure psychiatric units, and seven private psychiatric units across London and the south-east, showed that 16 per cent of inpatients came from black and ethnic minority communities, although this group represented less than 4 per cent of the local population.

In forensic mental health services, meanwhile, the most deprived 20 per cent of the population have a fourfold higher admission rate compared to the remaining four-fifths.

Of the estimated 15,000 people in England with what the government describes as 'severe and enduring mental illness', between 14 and 200 per 100,000 are defined as 'difficult to engage'. This group is more likely to live in inner-city areas, to be homeless, and is over-represented in suicide, violence and murder cases. Around half have traditionally lost contact with specialist mental health services, leaving GPs to provide continuity of care. Up to a third are likely to move out of their locality within a year.

# 3. The structure of mental health services

Most of the old long-stay psychiatric beds have now closed, and the number of residential places available in the community for people with mental illness has risen. Though nine out of 10 patients with a mental health problem are managed in primary care, around 80 per cent of NHS spending supports inpatient services. New structures are developing to commission and run mainstream mental health services in the community, involving closer joint working between primary healthcare and social services, pooled budgets, and the future formation of care trusts.

## Who commissions care?

English and Welsh health authorities, Scottish health boards and Northern Ireland's health and social services boards have commissioned most mental health services since the creation of the purchaser/provider split more than a decade ago. High and medium-security services, and other highly specialist mental health services, are commissioned at regional level.

Local authority social services departments commission social care for people with mental health problems, including residential care. Different bodies, namely local authorities, the Benefits Agency and the Department for Education and Employment, administer other relevant services such as housing, welfare benefits and employment services respectively.

In many areas there are close links between health and local authority commissioners; joint commissioning of mental health services is becoming more common, and this trend towards closer working is central to government policy for the future.

Generally speaking, responsibility for health services commissioning is being devolved to primary care trusts in England. These are large groups of general practices formed from the merging of primary care groups. PCTs now have greater responsibility and power to handle budgets and provide as well as commission services. In Wales, local health groups, which are coterminous with local authority boundaries, are set to become the lead commissioning body after the abolition of five existing Welsh health authorities. There are no plans to devolve commissioning of mental health services from health board level in Scotland and Northern Ireland.

The national service framework for mental health (see page 37) was published by the Labour government in 1998. It states that HAs will retain responsibility for commissioning certain mental health services. These will include medium and high-security services, services for eating disorders, mother and baby units, early dementia and gender dysphoria services, which should also continue to be provided by specialist mental health trusts.

But the framework also says that local health and social care bodies need to evolve new models for commissioning mainstream mental health services. Possible options include the development of joint commissioning boards – including local authority, HA and PCG representatives; and 'lead commissioner'

models, whereby the PCT, HA or local authority would take the lead on commissioning. Pooled health and social care budgets are deemed a vital component of such arrangements.

Another option – the development of 'care trusts' – was outlined in the government's NHS plan, launched in July 2000. There is a lack of clarity about care trusts, mentioned twice in the plan, but with different models implied.

In the first model, care trusts are described as 'a new level of primary care trust', responsible for all local health and social care (including mental health services). Their purpose would be to provide even closer integration of health and social services, and to commission and be responsible for all local health and social service care.

In the other model, the term implies a closer integration of specialist mental health trusts and social care into bodies that would probably only provide services, rather than also commissioning.

## Who provides care?
### Adult services
Most of the old long-stay psychiatric beds associated with the days when mental health

services were organised around asylums have now been closed. In the 1950s there were an estimated 140,000 hospital inpatient beds in England, compared to roughly 38,000 now, as the box below shows.

The extent of bed closures varies geographically, with an almost three-fold variation by area in hospital bed provision per 100,000 population. But overall, nearly two-thirds of beds for people with mental illness are now situated outside NHS hospitals.

Alongside the fall in acute beds has been a rise in the number of residential places available in the community for people with mental illness. The number of registered, private mental health nursing homes rose by 43 per cent from 1994 to 1999. There is an estimated three-fold variation in numbers of residential places between HAs.

Acute inpatient provision now deals mainly with patients with severe mental illness. Community and primary care services have absorbed much of the day-to-day management of less severe mental health problems. Indeed it has been estimated that 90 per cent of patients with a mental health problem are managed entirely in primary care, even though around 80 per cent of spending on NHS mental health supports inpatient services.

So it is the primary healthcare team – whose core members are GPs, practice nurses, health visitors and district nurses – which deals with most mental health cases, even if it then refers them on to specialist providers.

## Beds for people with mental illness in England, 1997-8

### NHS hospital beds

| | |
|---|---|
| Total | 37,880 |
| Children | 520 |
| Short-stay elderly | 7,380 |
| Long-stay elderly | 7,410 |
| Others: short-stay | 14,460 |
| Others: long-stay | 4,910 |
| Others: secure unit | 1,920 |
| Residential | 1,280 |

### Private nursing homes/hospitals

| | |
|---|---|
| Total | 28,280 |
| Elderly | 19,130 |
| Others (including children) | 9,150 |

### Staffed residential home places

| | |
|---|---|
| Total | 35,980 |
| Elderly | 21,040 |
| Others | 14,940 |

### Small registered residential home places

| | |
|---|---|
| Total | 2,580 |

| **Overall total** | **104,720** |

*Source: Department of Health.*
*Figures are for England only*

In England, specialist mental health trusts provide a full range of services, including acute inpatient care and community mental health services, along with rehabilitation services, residential care centres, drop-in facilities and the like. Joint mental health and learning disabilities trusts are fairly common.

Community mental health teams work alongside community nursing teams, and sometimes this pattern is reflected in management terms by the development of joint community and mental health trusts – this is the usual model of provision in Wales, for example. Mental health, community and primary care are jointly managed in Scotland's primary care trusts.

Community mental health teams encompass a range of professionals, the most obvious being community psychiatric nurses and approved social workers. They can vary widely in their composition, with some more heavily populated by nurses or social workers and vice versa. The average population covered by a community mental health team was 60,000 in 1996/97. At that time, only around 10 per cent of services had a specialised team offering assertive outreach or intensive support; a similar proportion had a crisis team. The NHS plan seeks to build on such interventions (see page 42 for more details).

Social care for people with mental health problems is provided partially by local authority social services departments, although most residential care is provided by the independent sector – both private concerns and the voluntary sector. Recent years have seen a push towards improved integration between HAs and social services departments in terms of the provision as well as the commissioning of mental health services. Somerset Partnership NHS and Social Care trust has been hailed as an example of the way forward in the NHS plan, as the box below shows.

### Integrated working in Somerset: a possible care trust model

Somerset Partnership NHS and Social Care trust, England's first integrated health and social care trust, began in April 1999. The trust is the result of a merger between the former mental health and learning disabilities trust and the mental health element of the local social services department. Social workers and other mental health staff are still local authority employees, but are managed alongside NHS staff by the trust, which has a former social worker as its chief executive.

Mental health services are commissioned jointly across the patch, via a board made up of local authority, HA and PCT representatives. This puts Somerset in a strong position to develop one of England's first wave of 'care trusts', whatever model for the future emerges (see pages 18 and 43).

One possible scenario of the 'care trust' concept is that bodies following Somerset's model would eventually become the norm.

## Specialist/secure care

There are three special hospitals for England and Wales – Ashworth, Rampton and Broadmoor; and one for Scotland and Northern Ireland – The State Hospital at Carstairs. The units cater for patients with mental illness, personality disorders or learning disabilities, or often a combination of these disorders.

These patients' behaviour can be very dangerous; many have committed serious offences and have a high public profile. The hospitals therefore have a dual role, combining security and therapy.

Special or 'high-security' hospitals are defined as being 'for persons who are liable to be detained under the Mental Health Act 1983 and… require treatment under conditions of high security on account of their dangerous, violent or criminal propensities'.

The *Fallon Inquiry*, commissioned by the NHS Executive and published in 2000, stated that the special hospitals 'have clear twin security and therapeutic objectives. The security objectives include the protection of the public, by seeking to ensure that patients do not escape or abscond, and the provision of a safe environment for staff and patients within the hospitals. The therapeutic objectives include the need to do everything possible to provide therapy for patients so that their illness/disorder can be treated and their behaviour made less dangerous for others and themselves'.

In terms of security, the three English hospitals have experienced no escapes or absconders from leaves of absence since 1997. Therapeutically, the story is less certain. In 1999, inspectors found a sorry lack of reliable information about attempts to treat and rehabilitate patients, with the limited data available suggesting that each patient is, on average, engaged in one episode of 'activity' per day – such as therapy, workshops, access to fresh air, internal shopping.

There is some innovation in the treatment of patients with personality disorder, however. For example, in terms of inpatient care, Aylesbury's Grendon Prison treats personality-disordered offenders in what it describes as a 'therapeutic community'. The underlying philosophy of care is that personality disorder is a disorder of relationships – with victims, family and the self. Working with a multidisciplinary team including prison officers, forensic psychologists, psychodynamic psychotherapists and probation officers, residents are encouraged to see when and why they became abusive and when and why they have been abused; and to make the link between being a victim and making a victim.

On an outpatient level, meanwhile, Dorset Healthcare trust runs an intensive psychological therapy outpatient service for personality-disordered patients. Many of the service's patients are para-suicidal, engage in self-harming behaviour, and have considerable difficulty managing their emotions and relationships. They are offered psychotherapy on an individual and group basis, often for between nine and 12 months.

*Services for children and adolescents*

Child and adolescent psychiatrists treat children and young people either on an inpatient or outpatient basis, in hospitals or child guidance centres. The preferred practice is for the patient to remain in their home environment, however, in some cases – especially if the home environment itself is contributing to the patient's condition – they may need to stay in hospital.

Children and adolescents are usually admitted to general children's wards in hospitals, rather than adult wards. The only exception is meant

*The preferred practice is to care for children in their own homes; they are only hospitalised when necessary.*

to be if the admission is an emergency and no alternative is available, as spelt out in the code of practice in the 1983 Mental Health Act.

Social workers are often part of the sectioning process, and are often part of child guidance teams. Local education authorities employ education welfare officers to monitor pupils with problems. Some local education authorities also employ educational psychologists, who are specifically trained to deal with emotional and behavioural difficulties affecting children and young people.

Leading mental health charity Mind estimates that there are around 600 child guidance units throughout the UK. These units are multi-professional centres where psychiatrists, social workers, psychologists, child psychotherapists, occupational and other therapists work together, often on a sessional basis, to improve child and adolescent mental health. Clients are normally referred by a GP, social worker or educational welfare officer.

Therapeutic communities can provide residential accommodation for young people, normally over the age of 13, with severe emotional problems and/or highly disturbed behaviour. These centres are often the last resort before housing in a secure unit, and because of the high staff-to-client ratio are reckoned to be fairly successful.

Secure accommodation in community homes is offered for children under 18 whose behaviour is so disturbed that they represent a real danger to themselves or others; and for the small group of young people sentenced to long periods of detention after committing very serious crimes. There are 350 secure beds of this kind in 40 units across England.

## Structures to oversee quality

Primary care groups and local health groups in Wales are accountable to HAs. English HAs and trusts are accountable to the regional offices of the NHS Executive, which is part of the Department of Health. Their Welsh, Scottish and Northern Irish equivalents report to their respective national governments.

The DoH oversees the quality of NHS services. In 1999 the Labour government set up the Commission for Health Improvement to monitor NHS activity and ensure best possible standards are achieved. It is playing a lead role in promoting clinical governance – the system whereby all health organisations are expected to demonstrate continuously improving standards of care. Alongside the CHI, the National Institute for Clinical Excellence was established to assess and advise on which treatments work and are value for money for the NHS. The institute's brief includes ruling on controversial medical treatments such as drugs for the treatment of Alzheimer's disease.

*Neil O'Connor*

*Professor Louis Appleby has a brief to modernise and reform mental health services.*

The Mental Health Act Commission conducts independent inspections of mental health facilities – in 1996 it visited 47 per cent of acute adult psychiatric inpatient units in England and Wales. The Scottish equivalent is called the Mental Welfare Commission.

The government's national director for mental health or mental health czar has a brief to 'spearhead the government's drive to modernise and reform mental health services'. At the time of writing in 2001 the czar was Manchester University psychiatry professor Louis Appleby (pictured on page 23).

Local authorities are accountable through the local government elections. The Social Services Inspectorate, part of the DoH, assists local government, voluntary and private bodies in the planning and delivery of social care services. It runs a national inspection programme, evaluating the quality of services experienced by users and carers (see box, left).

A General Social Care Council for England is due to be established in October 2001. Equivalent bodies for Wales, Scotland and Northern Ireland are also in the pipeline. The GSCC's role will be to act as the guardian of standards for the social care workforce. This will include drawing up codes of practice for social care workers and their employers; registering the workforce; and taking over the regulation of professional social work education and training from the Central Council for Education and Training in Social Work.

## Social Services Inspectorate standards

The SSI inspects compulsory mental health admissions against the following set of standards:

- Users assessed under the Mental Health Act receive an appropriate response through hospital admission and/or services to support them in the community.

- Social services department makes clear arrangements for assessment of people with mental health problems under the act and instigates actions to meet assessed needs.

- Users who are or may be detained under the act have access to care programme approach and/or care management systems which provide support through keyworking, monitoring and review.

- SSD works collaboratively with other agencies and other local authority departments to ensure a co-ordinated approach to services.

- Referral, assessment, care planning and service provision respect the rights of people compulsorily detained and are provided in a non-discriminatory way.

- SSD staff are given appropriate training and support.

- SSD management arrangements support provision of a mental health service which incorporates the needs of people who are or may be detained under the act.

The DoH has also announced proposals to establish a Social Care Institute for Excellence in the summer of 2001. According to the DoH, the role of this institute will be to review research and practice to create a knowledge base of what works in social care, with information being made available to managers, practitioners and users.

# 4. How mental health services are delivered

Under the care programme approach all patients receiving specialist mental healthcare should be given a systematic assessment of their health and social care needs, a key worker and a written care plan. Care is delivered by a multidisciplinary team, typically comprising psychiatrists, clinical psychologists, mental health nurses, mental health social workers and therapists. Moves are afoot to integrate CPA and social services care management, with one lead officer. Two types of CPA are envisaged, standard and enhanced.

## Primary care

Around 90 per cent of patients with mental health problems are estimated to be managed entirely within primary care – which is staffed by professionals with only limited training in mental health issues.

GPs are fully qualified doctors and as such are expected to follow a career-long programme of continuing professional development, but they are by necessity generalists. After they have qualified there is no specific compunction for them to receive any mental health training beyond what they learn during their undergraduate training and during the general practice year.

Few practice nurses have received training to provide mental health services, either. While the community nursing team is likely to be trained to spot and deal with particular mental illnesses – for example, health visitors identifying mothers with postnatal depression or district nurses helping patients deal with bereavement – none of these groups has training covering the management of patients with schizophrenia or depression, for example.

Some GP practices employ counsellors – one 1998 study suggested that as many as 40 per cent of surgeries did so.

But for most people with mental illness, their initial contact with statutory services is made via a consultation with a GP.

The box below shows the number of patients with various forms of mental illness that a typical GP might expect to encounter in a given year.

## Number of mentally ill patients per GP list of 1,900

| Diagnosis | Annual prevalence |
|---|---|
| Mixed anxiety and depression | 87 |
| Alcohol dependence | 53 |
| Generalised anxiety | 36 |
| Drug dependence | 25 |
| Depressive episode | 24 |
| Obsessive compulsive disorder | 14 |
| All phobias | 13 |
| Panic disorder | 9 |
| Psychotic illness | 5 |
| All neuroses | 182 |

*Source: OPCS survey of psychiatric morbidity report (1995)*

It has been estimated that GPs diagnose just under half of mental health problems. A combination of drug and 'talking' treatments are the main weapons in their armoury; GPs refer roughly a quarter of the patients they have diagnosed as having mental health problems to other professionals.

## Community care

GPs refer roughly 24 patients per 1,000 population annually to specialist mental health services – that is, mental health services provided to inpatients (in hospitals) and patients living in the community by anyone from psychiatrists and psychologists to mental health social workers and counsellors.

Since 1991, the care programme approach has set out the means by which services for people with mental health problems, provided by any specialist psychiatric provider, are delivered across England. Similar but less formal systems apply across the rest of the UK.

The CPA states that all mental health patients should receive a thorough and systematic assessment of their health and social care needs, and, flowing from that, a written care plan. They should have a keyworker or 'care co-ordinator', and should undergo regular reviews of all their care needs.

The CPA was introduced as a way to improve and standardise the delivery of community care services. As such, most health authorities introduced the approach for all inpatients being considered for discharge, and for all new patients accepted by specialist psychiatric services after April 1991.

In practice, however, if patients were not considered 'vulnerable' or to have particularly complex needs, decisions about after-care, and details of the after-care itself, would often not be recorded. Such patients would also not become part of the central CPA register – which lists those patients considered to be at risk, and names their care co-ordinator and the timing of reviews. Definitions of 'vulnerability', and approaches to adoption of the CPA – whether or how the introduction of the CPA has been 'tiered', for example – varies by HA.

Care management, which developed alongside the CPA, is local authority rather than NHS-led. It has been used where individuals have complex needs for care and treatment; the care manager co-ordinates the care provided for each service user, including social and physical healthcare needs as well as emotional and psychological ones.

After several high-profile murder cases where lack of co-ordination between the various agencies involved in care provision was identified as a contributory factor, moves towards integrating NHS and social services' inputs was accelerated.

## Integrating the CPA

Current policy is, therefore, for health and local authorities to work together and develop an integrated system of CPA and care management, including:

- a single operational policy;

- joint training for health and social care staff;

- one lead officer to act as care co-ordinator;

- common risk assessment and management policy;

- shared information system across health and social care;

- single complaints procedure;

- agreement on allocation of resources, and devolved budgets where possible;

- joint serious incident process;

- one point of access for health and social care assessments, and co-ordinated care.

All health and social services departments have to identify a lead officer, whose role is to ensure an integrated approach across all agencies; extra resources needed for the proposed co-ordination of services have been made available, through the mental health grant.

The CPA is now being streamlined into two levels. The standard CPA is for individuals who need the support of only one agency or discipline, who pose no danger to themselves or others, and would not be at high risk if they lost contact with services. The enhanced CPA is for people with multiple needs, who need to be in contact with more than one agency and/or professional. Such patients might have several clinical conditions and/or mental health problems. They may also be identified as hard to engage and could pose a risk to themselves or others if they lost contact with mental health services.

Risk management is considered a key element of the CPA, and crisis and contingency plans must now be included in care planning for those on the enhanced CPA.

There are a variety of models for community mental health provision, and services vary enormously due to factors including geography, funding, the nature of historical provision, and the availability of staff.

## Acute and specialist care

Of the 100 patients diagnosed by a typical GP as having a mental health problem each year, only a handful will spend time as an inpatient in a psychiatric hospital.

As the availability of acute mental health beds has diminished along with the closure of the Victorian asylums, the utilisation of new and remaining beds has become much more intensive. Department of Health figures

suggest the number of hospital bed days taken up by people with mental illness fell by 20 per cent between 1992/93 and 1998/99. Five of the ten most heavily occupied bed categories in English hospital wards are those occupied by patients with mental illness. (See box, below).

### Top 10 bed categories by occupancy level

| Ward type | Occupancy level (%) |
|---|---|
| 1. Mental illness: short stay | 90.8 |
| 2. Mental illness: secure unit | 90.3 |
| 3. General/acute: elderly, normal care | 89.4 |
| 4. Learning disabilities: long stay | 87.8 |
| 5. Mental illness: long stay | 87.3 |
| 6. Learning disabilities: children, long stay | 86.0 |
| 7. Mental illness: elderly, long stay | 84.7 |
| 8. Learning disabilities: short stay | 84.7 |
| 9. Mental illness: elderly, short stay | 84.0 |
| 10. General/acute: other | 83.3 |
| **Overall average occupancy** | **82.5** |

Source: Department of Health

## How many people are admitted?

Around 250,000 voluntary inpatient admissions – that is, admissions into NHS and private mental health facilities where patients have agreed to treatment without being legally compelled to do so – occur each year. By 1998-99 the number of formal (involuntary) – admissions to NHS facilities and private mental nursing homes per year had risen to 27,079 – a jump of 69 per cent over the previous decade. Ninety three per cent of these admissions were under Part II of the 1983 Mental Health Act. This means that patients are compulsorily admitted in the interests of their own health or safety, or for the protection of other people. Most of the other formal admissions, a total of 1,900 in 1998-99, were of people involved in criminal proceedings.

A total of nearly 13,000 patients were detained under the act at 31 March 1999, and of these, 10 per cent were in high-security hospitals, of which there are three in England and one in Scotland. Of these patients, 65 per cent were classified as having mental illness, 28 per cent psychopathic disorder and 6 per cent either mental impairment or severe mental impairment.

The average length of stay of a patient in a high-security hospital is seven to eight years. Among the most serious offenders admitted during the years 1989-98, 26 per cent had been charged with or convicted of homicidal offences (murder, attempted murder, threat or conspiracy to murder, manslaughter, infanticide); 37 per cent other violent offences; 9 per cent sexual offences; 12 per cent property offences; 7 per cent other offences; and 9 per cent no offences.

## Guardianship

A total of 632 new cases of guardianship under the Mental Health Act – a system whereby a patient is provided with a guardian on the recommendation of two doctors and after an application by an approved social worker – arose in the year to 31 March 2000. In 99 per cent of cases, guardianship was conferred on a local authority rather than a named person. Guardians can require a patient to live in a specified place and attend specified places for treatment, occupation and education and training. Guardianship orders last for six months, and are renewable for a further six months and then a year at a time.

## Mental health staff

There are many categories of staff specifically trained to care for people with mental illness, each with their own separate training, qualifications and professional standards. There were 7,206 psychiatrists in England in September 1999, according to the latest figures. Of these, 2,808 were consultants, 2,762 were doctors in training and the rest were working in other grades, including staff grade, associate specialist and clinical assistant posts. Almost two-thirds of these doctors worked in general psychiatry, with 11 per cent working in child and adolescent psychiatry, a further 11 per cent in old-age psychiatry, and smaller numbers specialising in learning disabilities,

*Health visitors initially identify and deal with mothers who have postnatal depression, like this one with her crying baby, but many patients need more specialist care.*

forensic psychiatry and psychotherapy. There were just under 36,000 nurses working in psychiatry and a further 8,400 in learning disabilities in England in September 2000.

More than 4,000 clinical psychologists work in the NHS, along with around 400 psychotherapists and 450 art/music and drama therapists. Around 4,800 'approved' social workers work in England and Wales, averaging 30 per local authority. In July 2000 the UK had 21,061 state-registered occupational therapists.

*Psychiatrists*

Psychiatrists are medical doctors trained in a range of sciences, including sociology, psychology and biomedical sciences. After qualification as a doctor, they undertake general professional training for three years, usually gaining experience of child and adolescent psychiatry, old-age psychiatry and psychotherapy. Consultant psychiatrists will have typically completed six years' undergraduate and seven years' post-graduate experience before appointment to a substantive post.

Psychotherapy is one of a psychiatrist's main forms of treatment, although most psychiatrists now work within a multidisciplinary team. This means they practise alongside other practitioners, especially clinical psychologists, to provide a full range of therapies and in a variety of formats. Within this context, psychiatrists tend to be responsible for the more complex patients, especially those with a psychiatric history and, perhaps, repeated suicide attempts and/or inpatient admissions.

*Clinical psychologists*

Clinical psychologists are psychology graduates who have trained for a further three years in a range of applied psychological skills, and gained a doctorate of clinical psychology. Their training, normally funded by the NHS Executive, centres on the application of the science of psychology in therapeutic work with a range of different client groups and in a variety of settings.

Once qualified, clinical psychologists work with individuals, couples, families and groups, in settings including hospital wards, day centres, prisons, rehabilitation units, community mental health teams and in primary care. Clinical psychologists' average number of contacts per patient episode is seven, and the average duration of an episode

is over four months. They accept referrals from GPs, psychiatrists, social workers and other professionals; and work with people of all age groups and varying severities of mental health problem. They also work with people with learning disabilities, physical and sensory handicaps, brain injuries, alcohol or drug problems and a range of physical health problems.

## Mental health nurses

After completing the common foundation programme that takes up the first 18 months of all nurses' training, fledgling mental health nurses specialise in mental health nursing for a further 18 months, combining further academic training with relevant work placements. Mental health nurses work mainly in community settings, as part of community mental health teams; others work on acute mental health inpatient wards and small numbers in forensic mental health.

## Mental health social workers

Social workers who work in mental health are called approved social workers in England, Wales and Northern Ireland, and 'mental health officers' in Scotland. Approved social workers are experienced social workers who have undergone further training to enable them to carry out statutory responsibilities under mental health legislation.

---

### Mental health prescribing

There are three main categories of mental health drugs prescribed in the NHS:

- Hypnotics and anxiolytics (also know as anti-anxiety drugs or minor tranquillisers), including benzodiazepines such as Valium;

- Antidepressants, including tricyclic antidepressants such as amitriptyline and the newer selective serotonin reuptake inhibitors, such as Prozac;

- Anti-psychotics (also known as major tranquillisers) such as Largactil, which are used to treat conditions such as schizophrenia and manic depression.

Latest figures show that in 1999, doctors issued more than 20 million prescriptions for antidepressants, 16 million for hypnotics and anxiolytics and nearly 6 million for anti-psychotics; at a total net ingredient cost of more than £430m.

## Five examples of mental health beacons

### Bedfordshire and Luton Community NHS trust assertive outreach service

The trust runs a court diversionary scheme for Bedfordshire, which aims to ensure that all patients discharged from secure services or the judicial system receive care, support and continual monitoring of their progress. A team of specially trained community mental health nurses and social workers runs the service, working closely with the probation service, police and voluntary sector.

### Wolverhampton Afro-Caribbean community initiative

This initiative provides day care, outreach services and supported housing for members of the Afro-Caribbean community with mental illness. The service is provided by the voluntary sector but funded through social services in partnership with the NHS. The aim is for project workers and volunteers to maintain contact with people who have serious mental illness, who might otherwise lose touch with mainstream services.

### Camden and Islington Community NHS trust – Drayton Park women's crisis project

This project offers an alternative to hospital accommodation for up to 12 women in mental health crisis (and up to four children). The design of the service was based on the views of women service users and the professionals who work with them. Staff offer 24-hour support, assessment, up to four weeks' residence and a range of service options and treatments. Staff also work with community workers and encourage them to continue regular contact with women while at the centre, to ensure continuity of care after they leave.

### Avon and Western Wiltshire Mental Healthcare trust family work for schizophrenia service

Although there is a large body of evidence showing that interventions with families of people with schizophrenia are effective in reducing relapse rates, such care has been difficult to incorporate into mainstream clinical practice. Here, a 'service champion' ensures family work for schizophrenia is integrated into everyday practice and is offered to all families for whom it is appropriate. A clear referral process links inpatient wards with community mental health teams and makes the service accessible to primary care and voluntary agencies. Training is offered to all disciplines.

### Barrow community gym

Barrow-in-Furness, a deprived town in the north-west of England, has high levels of mental ill health. Barrow's primary care group has identified mental health as one of its priorities and opened a town centre gym accessible to many different referral agencies. Involvement from users includes volunteering in all aspects of delivering and evaluating the service, from fitness buddying to leaflet design. There is also an employment project to enable users to access employment for one year.

They are trained in areas such as models of, approaches to, and methods of treatment for mental disorder; and risk assessment and management. Their role is essentially to work to protect the interests of people with mental disorder. Approved social workers are often involved in planning, negotiating and managing compulsory admissions to hospital, after considering all possible alternatives.

Local authorities commission higher-education institutions to train approved social workers for them, with quality standards set by the Central Council for Education and Training in Social Work.

### Therapists

Occupational therapists usually qualify after completing a three-year OT degree (four years in Northern Ireland). There is also a four-year part-time option, and a two-year accelerated route for graduates in other disciplines. Once qualified, OTs work in psychiatric units, day hospitals and in the community, and may be employed by a health authority, a social services department or a voluntary organisation. They work with mentally ill people to help them build up the confidence and skills necessary for personal, social, domestic, leisure or work activities.

Art, drama, music and dance therapists are often graduates in their chosen discipline, who undertake further training to help them enable mentally ill people to express themselves and communicate through the arts.

*Occupational therapists can undertake further training to enable people with mental illness to express themselves through art.*

# 5. Government policy on mental health

New Labour has taken a three-pronged approach to policy on mental health services – standard-setting, in the form of the national service framework on mental health; structural reform and inward investment, in the shape of new arrangements as outlined in the NHS plan; and legislative change, in the form of a white paper proposing reform of the 1983 Mental Health Act.

## The national service framework

National service frameworks are the government's preferred method for setting the clinical standards to which the NHS must work. Mental health was one of the first two frameworks drawn up by the government for England – the other related to the treatment of coronary heart disease.

The framework focuses on the mental health needs of working age adults, that is, people aged 16-65, and sets out seven national standards for mental health services (see box on page 38, overleaf).

*People with drink problems have a higher-than-average rate of mental health problems.*

Jon Walter

## National service framework standards

### Mental health promotion

#### Standard 1

Health and social services should:

* promote mental health for all, working with individuals and communities;
* combat discrimination against individuals and groups with mental health problems, and promote their social inclusion.

### Primary care and access to services

#### Standard 2

Any service user who contacts their primary healthcare team with a common mental health problem should:

* have their mental health needs identified and assessed;
* be ordered effective treatments, including referral to specialist services if required.

#### Standard three

Anyone with a common mental health problem should be able to:

* contact round the clock the local services to meet their needs and receive adequate care;
* use NHS Direct, as it develops, for first-level advice and referral on to specialist helplines or to local services.

### Effective services for people with severe mental illness

#### Standard four

All service users on the CPA should:

* receive care which optimises engagement, prevents or anticipates crisis, and reduces risk;
* have a copy of a written care plan that includes the action to be taken in a crisis

by service users, their carers, and care co-ordinators; advises the GP how to respond if the service user needs additional help; is regularly reviewed by the care co-ordinator;

* be able to access services 24 hours a day, 365 days a year.

#### Standard five

Each service user assessed as requiring a period of care away from home should have:

* timely access to an appropriate hospital bed or alternative bed or place, which is in the least restrictive environment consistent with the need to protect them and the public; and is as close to home as possible;
* a copy of a written after-care plan agreed on discharge, setting out care and rehabilitation to be provided, identifying the care co-ordinator, and specifying action to be taken in a crisis.

### Caring about carers

#### Standard six

All people who provide regular and substantial care for a person on the care programme approach should:

* have their own caring, physical and mental health needs assessed at least annually
* have their own written care plan.

### Preventing suicide

#### Standard seven

Local health and social care communities should prevent suicides by:

* meeting standards 1-6;
* supporting local prison staff in preventing suicides among prisoners;
* ensuring staff are able to assess suicide risk;
* developing local systems for suicide audit.

To support agencies in meeting these standards, the framework identifies local action and national 'underpinning' programmes to enable implementation. These include finance; workforce planning, education and training; research and development; clinical decision support systems and information. The framework also sets a series of national milestones along with performance indicators.

The framework has five main focuses. Rather than specify structural changes expected to deliver its goals, it calls on local health and social care agencies to put in place their own systematic and sustainable programmes of change management, working to suggested service models.

## 1. Social exclusion and mental health

The first focus is on mental health promotion. This reflects a recognition by the government that mental health problems can result from a range of adverse factors associated with social exclusion, and can in itself, in turn, be a cause of it:

- Unemployed people are twice as likely as those in work to suffer from depression.

- Children in the poorest households are three times more likely to have mental health problems.

- Half of all women and a quarter of all men will be affected by depression during some period in their lives.

- Victims of abuse or domestic violence have higher rates of mental health problems.

- People with drug and drink problems have higher rates of mental health problems.

- Between a quarter and a half of people who sleep rough have a serious mental disorder.

- Some black and ethnic minority communities have higher rates of mental health problems.

- There is a high rate of mental health problems among people in prison.

- People with physical illnesses have twice the rate of mental health problems.

The framework calls on health authorities, hospital trusts, primary care groups, primary care trusts and local authorities to develop effective mental health promotion for:

- whole populations, through initiatives to promote healthy schools, workplaces and neighbourhoods;

- individuals at risk, by supporting new parents and unemployed people for example;

- vulnerable groups, including specific programmes for groups such as black and ethnic minority communities, homeless people, and people with alcohol and drug problems, for example.

It also calls for action to combat discrimination against people with mental health problems and promote positive images of mental ill health.

### 2. Improving primary care

The second focus is on improving primary care and access to services. The framework recognises that most healthcare is provided by the primary healthcare team, and suggests ways to build capacity and capability to manage common problems and refer on for specialist advice, assessment and care. Proposals include:

- use of protocols, with depression as the first priority, followed by postnatal depression, eating disorders, anxiety disorders and schizophrenia. The National Institute for Clinical Excellence may be called upon to review locally developed protocols and, where appropriate, 'kitemark' examples of good practice.

- management of referrals to specialist services, including psychological therapies, and monitoring waiting times;

- primary care liaison and training by specialist mental health services staff;

*Laurence Bulaitis*

*Carers play a vital role in helping people with mental health problems, including representing their interests.*

- support for patients and their families in understanding their mental health problems and treatment, and in contacting local self-help groups.

The framework also states that local health and social care communities need to establish explicit and consistent arrangements for 24-hour access to services. This can be via the GP or primary healthcare team; through NHS Direct and other helplines; in A&E departments through mental health liaison services; with a gateway to specialist services through effective out-of-hours arrangements; and including people detained by the police.

### 3. Severe mental illness

The third focus is on improving services for people with severe mental illness. Here, the central aim should be the integration of the care programme approach and care management, and the full implementation of the new arrangements for standard and enhanced CPA (see chapter four). Other approaches should include:

- implementing arrangements for the assessment and care of people detained by police, brought before a court or in prison;

- ensuring staff are competent to assess the risk of violence or self-harm, to manage people who may become violent, and to know how to assess and manage risk;

- implementing local protocols for the effective and safe care of people with severe mental illness;

- engaging service users who would be at risk if they lost contact with services, through assertive outreach and effective medication;

- integrating crisis prevention and management;

- investing in a balance of hospital beds, staffed and supported accommodation, day places and home treatment.

*4. Caring about carers*

The fourth focus centres on recognising the vital role that carers play in helping people with mental health problems. This means ensuring that each carer's needs are assessed; that each carer receives easy-to-understand information about the help available to them, and about the services provided for the person for whom they are caring. There should be an annual, written care plan covering their caring, physical and mental health needs, and also educational and welfare needs for young carers.

*5. Preventing suicide*

The fifth focus is on preventing suicide, which is one of the target areas of the government's overall public health policy. Local health and social care communities are encouraged to help prevent suicides by delivering the service models outlined above, as well as:

- supporting prison staff in preventing suicides among prisoners and those on remand;

- ensuring staff are competent to assess the risk of suicide, especially among the most vulnerable people;

- developing local systems for suicide audit and learning lessons as appropriate.

## Scotland, Wales and Northern Ireland

Scotland produced a framework for mental health services in September 1997, with the aim of assisting staff in health, social work and housing agencies to develop a joint approach to the planning, commissioning and provision of integrated mental health services. The framework's overall aim was to generate consensus over the key issues in achieving transition from old-style psychiatric hospitals to more local, comprehensive mental health services.

Ministers established a mental health development fund amounting to an annual pump-priming investment of £3m for three years (1998/99 to 2000/01 inclusive), to help health boards develop new ways of working with trusts, GPs, local authorities and voluntary agencies and establish local community-focused services.

A broader local care partnership scheme was also set up, designed to assist with integration of health, housing and social care services for vulnerable groups. Under the framework, health boards assessed local needs, identified gaps in services and produced implementation plans covering the period 1998-2004.

Wales is due to produce its own mental health national service framework soon. This is expected to emphasise the further development of community mental health teams, rather than focus on other, more specialist teams.

Northern Ireland has no clear plans to produce such a framework, although in 2000 the government launched an ambitious action plan for mental health promotion across the province. This issued recommendations for all sectors of public life – including the early years, schools, youth, higher education, workplaces, health and social services and the media. It aimed to encourage the promotion of mental and emotional well-being. Mental health was also identified as a priority in the government's Investing for Health strategy consultation, which ended in April 2001.

## The NHS plan

The NHS plan, launched in July 2000, outlined the government's strategy for modernising the NHS in the 21st century. It envisaged an NHS 'redesigned around the needs of the patient' and promised to further devolve decision-making from the centre to local health services. The plan promised an extra £300m investment in mental health by 2003-4, to fast-forward the national service framework. This money will, the plan claims, be spent on a variety of new resources in primary and community care settings.

These include:

- 1,000 new graduate primary care mental health workers and 500 more community mental health staff to work with GPs and primary care teams, NHS Direct and hospital A&E departments;

- 50 early intervention teams aimed at reducing periods of untreated psychosis in young people;

- 335 crisis resolution teams;

- 50 new assertive outreach services to deal with high service users;

- Women-only day centres in every HA area;

- 700 new staff to take pressure off carers of mentally ill patients;

- 200 new long-term secure beds for patients inappropriately housed in high-security hospitals, and 400 staff to provide intensive support when such patients are discharged;

- 300 new staff working across health/prison services to improve mental health provision in hospitals;

- 140 new secure, and 75 specialist rehabilitation, hostel places for people with severe personality disorder.

The 1999 Health Act, which flowed from the 1997 *New NHS* white paper, created primary care trusts and brought in the statutory obligation to pursue clinical governance. It enabled local councils and the NHS to work more closely together by allowing the use of pooled budgets – that is, where either the local authority, HA or PCG takes the lead in commissioning services – and integrated provision, as in Somerset (see box on page 20). Under the NHS plan freedoms which already exist under the 1999 Health Act to enable the NHS and local authorities to work more closely together – including pooled budgets, lead commissioning and mergers – will become mandatory.

Local authorities, HAs and primary care groups/trusts will be eligible to receive incentive payments and reward joint working, either through the national performance fund in the case of health bodies, or through a social services fund of £50m rising to £100m from April 2003. PCGs have until April 2004 to become PCTs and the plan also introduces a further level of integration, in the form of 'care trusts' (see chapter three). These are single, multi-purpose bodies which will – depending on which interpretation is put on them – either commission and be responsible for all local health and social care, with social services care being delivered under delegated authority from local authorities; or merge specialist mental health trusts with the mental health functions of social services.

## Scotland's plan

*Our National Health*, Scotland's equivalent of the NHS plan, was published in December 2000. It pledged to accelerate implementation of the country's framework for mental health

## NHS plan targets for 2001/02

- By November 2001 each local implementation team should have signed off their stage 3 plan for implementing the national service framework and the mental health targets in the NHS plan; each health authority must reflect this plan in their planning for 2002-3 and beyond.

- By March 2002 each HA must have identified all clients who need the assertive outreach approach, and must have prepared plans for a further 50 assertive outreach teams, to ensure all clients who need this approach get it by 2003. The national psychiatric re-admission rate must also have been reduced to 12.3 per cent by the end of March.

- By March 2001 all users on enhanced CPA should have a written care plan, available on an electronic information system at all trust operational bases.

- By March 2002 this should be extended to cover all service users on CPA. The plans of enhanced CPA users must show plans to secure suitable employment or other occupational activity, adequate housing and entitlement to welfare benefits; all regular carers of people on enhanced CPA should have their own written care plan too.

- By the end of March 2001 all HAs should have in place protocols agreed between primary care and specialist mental health services for the management of depression and postnatal depression; anxiety disorders; schizophrenia; those requiring psychological therapies; and drug and alcohol dependence. HAs should review the operation of these protocols by the end of March 2002.

services, through an additional £2m for 2001-2 for projects linked to its agenda for improved care and access to care; and extra money for the mental illness specific grant.

Ministers also announced a further £4m for a campaign to promote positive mental health, and £5m to improve mental health hospitals. Quality initiatives have included quality indicators for mental health services, produced by the Scottish Health Advisory Service, a body that was set up in 1970 to prevent abuse or neglect of long-stay patients by inspecting NHS services and facilities.

The Clinical Standards Board – the Scottish equivalent of the English Commission for Health Improvement – is currently developing schizophrenia service standards.

In terms of mental health services for offenders, a 1999 policy set out a framework requiring care, custody, judicial and other agencies to work together on providing safe, seamless care – as far as possible in community-based accommodation – for forensic patients.

In February 2001 the Scottish Executive published an audit document, produced by the Scottish Development Centre for Mental Health, to help all mental health agencies identify their role in the care and custody of mentally disordered offenders and identify any gaps in current provision.

## Compulsory treatment outside hospitals
*Reforming the 1983 Mental Health Act*

In December 2000 the government brought out a white paper, *Reforming the 1983 Mental Health Act*. Under the 1983 act, powers to compulsorily treat patients apply only if they are detained in hospital. Especially given the huge shift of patients from hospital to community-based care, the government believes this makes the current legislation problematic, because clinicians have to wait until patients in the community become ill enough to need admission to hospital before compulsory treatment can be given.

The proposed new legislation would allow compulsory care and treatment to apply to patients outside hospital. It would be based on a broad definition of mental disorder covering 'any disability or disorder of mind or brain, whether permanent or temporary, which results in an impairment or disturbance of mental functioning'.

The white paper says use of compulsory powers 'will generally only be appropriate if a person is resisting care and treatment needed either in their best interests or because without care and treatment they will pose a significant risk of serious harm to other people'.

### Compulsory treatment orders

The basic procedure for using compulsory powers would be as follows:

* *Step one – preliminary examination*

Decisions to begin assessment and initial treatment would be based on a preliminary examination by two doctors and a social worker or other suitably trained mental health professional, having shown that the patient (a) needs further assessment or urgent treatment by specialist mental health services, and (b) without this might be at risk of serious harm or pose a similar risk to other people.

* *Step two – formal assessment/initial treatment*

Patient to receive a full assessment of their health/social care needs, and receive treatment set out in formal care plan up to a maximum of 28 days. After that, continuing use of compulsory powers would need to be authorised by the new mental health tribunal, a body set up under the 1983 Mental Health Act.

* *Step three – care and treatment order*

The tribunal, or court in the case of offenders, would be able to make a care and treatment order authorising the care and treatment specified in a care plan recommended by the clinical team. The first two orders could be up to six months each; and subsequent orders up to 12 months.

There would, the paper says, be clear criteria to define the circumstances in which compulsory powers could be used. The legislation would also set out the matters the clinical team should take into account when determining whether specialist mental health treatment is in the patient's best interests. There would be strict requirements for communication and disclosure of information about patients suffering from mental disorder, between health and social services and other agencies. Patients would, on the other hand, gain a new right of access to advice and support from independent specialist advocacy services, via the patient advocacy liaison service, which is scheduled to be introduced in 2002.

Other features of the legislation would include a new independent tribunal to determine all longer-term use of compulsory powers; safeguards for people with long-term mental incapacity; a new commission for mental health; and a statutory requirement to develop care plans.

Meanwhile, an expert committee has recently completed its review of Scotland's 1984 Mental Health Act. Its main findings are similar to those of its English counterpart, and the Scottish Executive pledged to produce legislative proposals in the summer.

# 6. Controversies in mental health services

Funding for drug treatments and workforce planning are issues that concern mental health campaigners. Charities also want the government to help change public attitudes, and to alter the emphasis on public safety in relation to compulsory detentions. The Commons health select committee proposed that compulsion should bring with it 'reciprocal obligations' to people with mental illness, and the government has now introduced a right to advocacy.

## The funding debate

Total annual mental health spending is currently more than £3bn and, at the time this book went to press, government claimed that in raising spending to this level it would have funded, by April 2001, an extra 500 secure beds, 320 staffed beds in NHS facilities and 220 assertive outreach services.

The Department of Health promised a further £300m by 2003-4 in the NHS plan. The Sainsbury Centre for Mental Health has pointed out that the timing of this funding will be crucial – a gradual rise over the three years would allow for sound financial planning and a sustainable investment in future service improvements.

Specific details on the staging of the mental health funding boost are unclear but, taken as a whole, the government's NHS increases are due to kick in at a rate of 8.5 per cent for 2001-2, then 6 per cent each for 2002-3 and 2003-4. If the mental health increases were to follow the same pattern, this would mean the £300m would split into £125m for 2001-2 and £87.5m each for 2002-3 and 2003-4.

The Sainsbury centre has also questioned whether the £300m figure is in addition to – or a continuation of – the £700m over three years that was attached to the national

*Steve Speller*

*Total annual mental health spending is currently more than £3bn with a further £3bn promised by 2003-4.*

service framework implementation. If the £300m is new money, the centre says considerable progress would be possible, although even then it questions whether it would be enough to fund the additional demands of the NHS plan. In terms of direct staff costs alone, the 8,000 new staff predicted as necessary to implement the government's reforms (see page 51) alone would cost, assuming an average salary of £25,000, around £200m. Capital, recruitment, training and management costs would be on top of that.

More generally, the House of Commons health select committee last year called on the health secretary to ensure that mental health services get their 'fair slice of the cake'. The committee also recommended that the DoH should monitor the very disparate levels of spending on mental health between health authorities and where necessary draw HAs' attention to spending which falls well below the national average. The government claimed monitoring already occurs, but pointed out that high spending does not necessarily equate to high quality.

One area of particular financial concern is the cost of mental health prescribing. New drugs in the field can be extremely expensive and there has been a good deal of publicity about the 'postcode prescribing lottery' caused by HAs rationing drugs such as Aricept, which is used to alleviate symptoms of Alzheimer's disease.

The National Institute for Clinical Excellence has the role of deciding whether or not new drug treatments should be provided on the NHS, but many service users doubt whether the really expensive drugs are really being given a fair hearing.

Atypicals for schizophrenia, for example – seen by many as a miraculous replacement for more traditional treatments with their notorious side-effects, such as tremors, shuffling and impotence – cost around £215 a month rather than £5 for the older drugs. It has been estimated that using atypicals as a first-line treatment would cost £200-£400m; quite a chunk out of the government's £700m funding for the framework. Leaked guidelines commissioned by the DoH last year suggested patients should not be given atypicals unless they had failed to respond to old-style drugs or suffered 'unacceptable' side-effects.

Even where drugs do receive NICE approval, funding can still be problematic. In the case of Aricept, which was approved in January 2001, for example, HAs each had to set aside an average of around £400,000 in anticipation of NICE's decision. Part of the justification for the cost-effectiveness of the drug was that it would keep patients out of nursing homes, bringing in the equivalent of £700,000 per HA in return – but this would be far from guaranteed, and could only occur at some indeterminate point in the future.

## Workforce issues

Workforce planning and recruitment and retention have long been the Achilles' heel of plans to improve mental health services. Latest figures suggest there are staff shortages across the board.

The Royal College of Psychiatrists' most recent recruitment survey found an overall vacancy rate of 12 per cent among consultant psychiatrist posts in England in 1999. In Wales and Scotland the rate was 8 per cent, and in Northern Ireland, 4 per cent.

Beneath these headline figures lay pockets of more serious recruitment difficulty, with vacancy rates of 17 per cent in rehabilitation psychiatry in England and Scotland, 16 per cent in substance misuse specialists in England, and 14-15 per cent in learning disability psychiatry in England, Scotland and Northern Ireland.

DoH figures suggest an overall vacancy rate of 7 per cent for psychiatrists in March 2000 – by far the highest vacancy rate of any medical or dental specialty, the overall average for which was under 3 per cent. In fact, six English trusts reported vacancy rates of more than 20 per cent; one of these had had a third of its psychiatric posts vacant for more than three months at the time of the survey. The DoH vacancy rate for mental health nurses was 4 per cent in March 2000 – just above the average for nurses as a whole. There were wide geographical variations underlying this figure, with rates approaching 9 per cent in London. Around 85 per cent of trusts reported problems in recruiting and retaining staff, according to one recent survey.

The Sainsbury Centre for Mental Health reports that there was a 10 per cent vacancy rate for full-time occupational therapy posts across the NHS, along with a drop of nearly half in applications for OT training courses.

The vacancy rate among approved social workers, as reported to the Association of Directors of Social Services, was 6 per cent in 1999. The global figure for all mental health staff was 7 per cent. There is an annual turnover of 10 per cent among approved social workers, and around half of social services departments –especially those in the north – report recruitment difficulties.

In recognition of existing problems and the additional workforce implications of the framework, the government established a national service framework workforce action team in December 1999. Its remit is 'to enable mental health services to ensure that their workforce is sufficient and skilled, well led and supported to deliver high-quality mental healthcare, including secure mental healthcare'.

WAT's interim report, published in September 2000, called for more investment in the mental health workforce, over and above the £2.5m for 230 extra psychiatry training posts and £4m for 300 mental health nurse training places already announced. Specifically, the team called for £2m to be invested in 55 clinical psychology training places and another £1m to train 52 community psychiatric nurses and 22 community nurses in mental health. It also set out 10 key areas of preparatory work feeding into its final report to ministers, due in the spring of 2001 but yet to appear as this book was being written.

The Sainsbury Centre for Mental Health has estimated that, taking into account both the framework and the NHS plan, a total of around 8,000 extra staff – a 12 per cent increase over the present workforce, and a total twice as large as that envisaged by the framework alone – will be needed.

The centre stresses that even assuming the right level of investment, the government faces an impossible task in reaching the number of doctors, psychologists, nurses and other staff required for several years yet. The centre says the government needs to develop a whole raft of new courses for various staff groups working in primary care, crisis resolution, early intervention, day centres, carer support and secure services. It says the DoH's workforce agenda should be wide-ranging and should include the imaginative use of family-friendly policies; the mature

### Training a future workforce

Staffordshire social services has responded to the workforce demands of the national service framework in three ways.

First, it has developed a programme of inter-agency training, bringing together people from social services, the NHS, police, probation, independent and voluntary agencies, and service users, to attend locally based training sessions which 'challenge the prejudices and stigma surrounding mental health'.

Second, it has launched a range of NVQ awards and distance learning projects to train mental health support workers for work with community care providers from the statutory and independent sectors.

And third, it has established an innovative in-house training scheme for approved social workers, which includes training from doctors and specialist trainers, and a module where service users participate as trainers, allowing candidates to learn 'first hand' from users willing to share their experiences.

workforce; skill mix and associated training plans; and pay flexibilities.

## Structural change

A survey of primary care groups conducted last year by the Sainsbury centre and the NHS Executive's London regional office raised questions about how well served mental health services might be if primary care trusts became responsible for commissioning mental health services.

The survey found that while three-quarters of PCGs had a named doctor who acted as clinical lead for mental health, only a third had a manager with responsibility for the area. Of these managers, more than 90 per cent spent less than a quarter of their time on mental health.

When asked about what strengths PCGs or PCTs could bring to the commissioning process, respondents cited joint working with the local authority and mental health trust; the creation of a locality focus in commissioning; and close links to primary care. But they admitted there could be attendant weaknesses, including a lack of resources; poor IT systems; and a tension between providing services for severely mentally ill people and those patients with common mental illnesses.

As for provision, 36 of the 197 PCGs said they expected to provide mental health services when they achieved trust status. The NHS plan signalled a shift in policy, meaning they may have less choice on the subject than they thought, however. While the framework approved the management of mental health services by PCTs under certain conditions only, the plan announced that PCTs would be rolled out nationally by 2004, with the first care trusts – potentially commissioning and providing all health and social care – gaining approval as early as 2001.

This goes against the recent trend for mental health services to merge into large specialist trusts, often covering more than one HA area, which some mental health experts have condemned as out of touch with local communities, and the unwelcome result of 'empire-building'.

Poor co-ordination between the NHS, social services and other agencies has been a theme running through the entire history of mental health services in the UK and, with this in mind, the government has attempted to redesign the structure of services as part of its modernisation programme.

The Commons health select committee has questioned whether the proposed reforms go far enough. In its 2000 report on mental health services, the committee argued for better co-operation between government departments over mental health issues, and called for a dedicated Cabinet mental health sub-committee to be established.

At a more local level, it called for the nation's health and social services organisations to be merged into single entities; and for closer working partnerships between health and social care agencies and other services, such as housing, substance misuse and learning disabilities services.

## Legal reform

The notion of compulsion has been the main area of controversy in the government's proposed reform of the 1983 Mental Health Act, first outlined in a green paper published in November 1999. While most mental health professionals, carers and even service users accept the need for compulsory powers in the community, there has been considerable concern that patients' rights must not be sacrificed on the altar of public safety.

In her evidence to the health select committee inquiry into mental health services held in the summer of 2000, Professor Genevra Richardson, who chaired the committee on whose work the green paper was based,

criticised the government for over-emphasising risks to public safety in its document. She agreed with the select committee chair David Hinchliffe that the government was 'in danger of chasing an agenda laid out by headlines in *The Sun*'.

In its report, the select committee emphasised that the possibility of compulsion must bring with it reciprocal obligations. This should include an obligation to provide services for those in mental distress so that compulsion is only ever a last resort, and an obligation to protect the civil rights of those who have been labelled with what is still seen as a stigmatising condition. It also called for the requirement that a patient is likely to benefit from the treatment proposed to be made much more explicit in the criteria for compulsion; and for a statutory right to advocacy.

The government's white paper, published in December 2000, retained public safety as its main thrust, but did make concessions such as introducing a new right to advocacy. Charities' calls for the new legislation to include a stronger reciprocal compulsion on health authorities to provide comprehensive services for users – for example making them guarantee to make assessments and provide the treatment promised in care plans – had little impact.

## Reform of secure services

It is generally accepted that the government's aim of increasing the capacity of the NHS to provide secure care on a local basis is a sound policy, but there has been much criticism over the lack of firm data on numbers of long and short-term medium and low-secure beds; and over the lack of rigorous assessment of patients' needs in the special hospitals.

The health select committee has also criticised the government's policy of merging the special hospitals with other mental health trusts – Ashworth with the Mental Health Services of Salford trust and Rampton with Central Nottinghamshire Healthcare trust, for example – in order to provide a more regional focus to care and management.

Indeed the committee – in line with the recommendations of the Fallon review following the Ashworth Inquiry – called for the closure of the three special hospitals and their gradual replacement with eight smaller, regionally based units, fully integrated with existing medium and low-secure and general mental health service provision.

Without such a radical approach, the committee argued, reform would not be workable because of 'their isolation, their difficulties in recruiting and retaining highly professional staff, and the culture which has developed within these institutions'.

## Cultural attitudes

Public attitudes on mental health and the perceived link between mental disorder and dangerousness are key areas in which mental health campaigners are keen to secure change.

The Sainsbury centre has described the inclusion of mental health promotion as a strand of the framework as 'an important milestone' in giving health and social services, for the first time, a clear remit to promote mental health for all and reduce the discrimination faced by people with mental health problems.

But last year the health select committee called on the government to take a more

*Cultural attitudes challenged by T-shirts and stickers at Mad Pride Festival, London 2000.*

proactive approach in challenging attitudes. It recommended a high-profile public campaign to educate the public about the realities of mental illness, and also a shift away from the government's own emphasis on risk when dealing with the media on mental health issues. It also pointed out that placing a greater value on users and carers by involving them more in service delivery could have the knock-on effect of challenging attitudes.

In March 2001 the government launched a £1m campaign, *Mind out for mental health*, aimed at challenging the discrimination faced by people with mental health problems.

A survey conducted as part of the campaign suggests the need for a change in attitudes is pressing. It found that only one third of young people aged 16-24 thought it was unacceptable to call people 'schizo' or 'psycho'. Twice as high a proportion felt it was wrong to use racist language. Although 61 per cent of respondents admitted to having used the words 'nutter', 'psycho', 'schizo' or 'loon', 51 per cent the word 'mental', and 44 per cent 'mad' to describe someone with a mental health problem, four-fifths agreed that having a mental health problem would lead to discrimination, and 55 per cent said they would not want anyone to know if they had a mental health problem.

# 7. The future of mental health services

The government has set a common agenda for local agencies to work to in partnership. The workforce implications are vast, as is the need for strong leadership. Though significant funding increases are promised, there is still competition from other hard-pressed services. Overall, the reform package holds up hope of significant progress, though not an overnight revolution.

So what does the future hold for mental health services in the UK? The consensus among mental health experts is that the government's progress in developing a comprehensive reform programme for mental health services has been impressive.

Rather than focusing on wholesale structural change, the national service framework and NHS plan have concentrated on setting a common agenda for a variety of local agencies to work to, in partnership.

For the first time, it offers the chance to develop a 'whole-systems' approach to mental healthcare, rather than a patchwork of disparately managed and delivered services. Mental health promotion, and its implicit non-acceptance of stigma around mental health issues, is a welcome feature. The development of mental health services in primary care and community settings, greater involvement of service users, and the growth of genuinely comprehensive services for patients with severe mental illness are all on the agenda. Overall, the reform package holds up hope of enormous progress.

But it is one thing writing down a plan which could hold all the answers, and another delivering the goods. The workforce implications of the government's plans are enormous, as will be the need for strong, well-informed leadership – often in fields such as primary care, where mental health knowledge has hitherto been scant.

And, as ever, money will be the key to success or failure. The costs of employing new staff and training them; of a new generation of mental health drugs and dissemination of good evidence about their use; and of the necessary improvements in hospital infrastructure will be huge.

So far the government has promised significant increases in funding. But while mental health has risen much higher up the pecking order of health priorities under this government than ever before, it must still compete with cancer, heart disease and waiting list initiatives for ministers' – and to an extent therefore, managers' – undivided attention.

Taken in context, one must also remember that while the UK's mental health expenditure takes up a similar proportion of overall health spending as in other developed countries, we still spend less on health than many of our European partners and other western economies.

The proposals will not mean an overnight revolution, then. But probably, over a 10-year

*Dan Atkin*

*The reform package holds hope of enormous progress for people with mental health problems.*

period, as the Sainsbury centre described the national service framework when it first appeared, this is 'the best chance in a generation for agencies and stakeholders to unite and move forward'.

## Further reading

Cohen A. *Primary care mental health. HSJ monograph no 2*. London: Emap Public Sector Management, 2000.

Jones, K. *A history of the mental health services*. London: Routledge, 1972.

Mind (the National Association for Mental Health) produces briefing papers on all aspects of mental health services in the UK. View or order online at www.mind.org.uk

*NSF Workforce Planning, Education and Training Underpinning Programme: Interim Report by Workforce Action Team*. Available via www.doh.gov.uk/mentalhealth

*Our National Health*. Available via www.scotland.gov.uk

*Provision of NHS Mental Health Services. House of Commons Select Committee on Health*. Fourth Report. July 2000. Available via www.parliament.uk/commons

*Reforming the Mental Health Act*. Available via www.doh.gov.uk/mentalhealth

*Report of the Review of Security at the High Security Hospitals,* February 2000. Available via www.doh.gov.uk

Sainsbury Centre for Mental Health executive briefings: *The NSF for Mental Health,* November 1999; *Taking your partners: using opportunities for inter-agency partnership in mental health,* March 2000; *Finding and keeping: review of recruitment and retention in the mental health workforce,* June 2000; *The implications of the NHS plan for mental health services,* September 2000; *Implementing standard one of the NSF,* January 2001. All available via www.scmh.org.uk

*The National Service Framework for Mental Health*. Available via www.doh.gov.uk/mentalhealth

*The NHS plan*. Available via www.doh.gov.uk/nhsplan

Timmins N. *The five giants: a biography of the welfare state*. London: Harper Collins, 1995.

## Glossary

Care trusts: single, multi-purpose bodies which will – depending on which interpretation is put on them – either commission and be responsible for all local health and social care, with social services care being delivered under delegated authority from local authorities; or merge specialist mental health trusts with the mental health functions of social services. The second model would probably only provide services.

Care programme approach: introduced in 1991, this set out a framework for health authorities, laying down how they should ensure people with mental health problems receive appropriate levels of support in the community, and relying on liaison between health and social care agencies. The CPA is now being streamlined at two levels: standard CPA for people who need the support of one agency or discipline and enhanced CPA for people with multiple needs.

Child guidance units: units where psychiatrists, psychologists, child psychotherapists, social workers, occupational and other therapists work together, often on a sessional basis, to improve child and adolescent mental health.

Clinical governance: the system whereby all health organisations are expected to demonstrate continuously improving standards of care.

Clinical Standards Board: the Scottish equivalent of the Commission for Health Improvement (see below).

Clinical psychologist: a psychology graduate who has trained for a further three years in a range of applied psychological skills, and gained a doctorate in clinical psychology.

Community mental health teams (CMHT): a range of professionals, including community psychiatric nurses and approved social workers, who work alongside community nursing teams and care for people with mental health problems.

Commission for Health Improvement (CHI): a statutory body set up in 1999 to monitor NHS activity and ensure the best possible standards are achieved.

Commission for Mental Health: a body to look after the interests of all people who are subject to care and treatment under the powers of the Reform of the 1983 Mental Health Act. It will monitor the use of formal powers and provide guidance on their operation and assure the quality of statutory training of practitioners.

Commissioning: an arrangement between primary care groups, or similar groups of health professionals, and hospitals or other providers of healthcare to provide health services for their population.

Enhanced CPA: see care programme approach.

Framework for mental health services: Scotland's equivalent of the national service framework for mental health.

General Social Care Council for England: (and its equivalents for Wales, Scotland and Northern Ireland) a body scheduled to be set up in October 2001 to act as the guardian of standards for the social care workforce. Its role to include: drawing up codes of practice for social care workers and their employers, registering the workforce and taking over the regulation of professional social work education and training from the Central Council for Education and Training in Social Work.

Guardianship: a system where a mental health patient is provided with a guardian on the recommendation of two doctors and after an application by an approved social worker. Guardianship is usually conferred on a local authority rather than a named person.

Involuntary admissions: patients compulsorily admitted into NHS and private mental health facilities in the interests of their own health or safety, or for the protection of other people.

Mental Health Act Commission: a government body that conducts independent inspections of mental health facilities (its Scottish equivalent is called the Mental Welfare Commission).

Mental health czar: the government's national director for mental health, with a brief to 'spearhead the government's drive to modernise and reform mental health services' – at the time this book was published the czar was Professor Louis Appleby of Manchester University .

Mental health nurse: a nurse who has completed the first 18 months of all nurse training and then specialised in mental health nursing for a further 18 months, through a combination of further training and work placements.

Mental health social worker: a social worker who has undergone further training to enable them to carry out statutory responsibilities under mental health legislation.

Mental health tribunal: a new body set up under the *Reforming the 1983 Mental Health Act* white paper.

National Institute for Clinical Excellence (NICE): a national body established in 1999 to assess and advise on which treatments work and are value for money for the NHS.

National service framework: a document outlining targets, guidelines and best practice in key clinical areas prepared by reviewing clinical evidence and consulting with experts.

NHS Direct: a national telephone helpline, staffed by nurses, to give advice and information to patients, with an online service also available.

NHS plan: the government's strategy for modernising the NHS in the 21st century, focusing on patient needs and devolving decision-making to local health services.

National service framework for mental health: the government's targets, guidelines and best practice in mental health; published in September 1999.

NSF workforce action team: formed by the government in December 1999 'to enable

mental health services to ensure that their workforce is sufficient and skilled, well led and supported to deliver high-quality mental health care, including secure mental healthcare'.

Psychiatrist: a qualified medical doctor who undertakes general professional training for three years, usually gaining experience of child and adolescent psychiatry, old age psychiatry and psychotherapy.

*Our National Health:* Scotland's equivalent of the NHS plan, published in December 2000, which included a pledge to accelerate implementation of the country's framework for mental health services.

Primary care group (PCG): a group of general practices covering a fixed geographical area, which has a single board and works together to commission health services for the local population.

Primary care trust (PCT): PCGs at level three or four, when the grouping of practices takes on greater responsibility and power to handle budgets and provide as well as commission services.

*Reforming the 1983 Mental Health Act:* December 2000 government white paper outlining changes so that compulsory care and treatment will apply to patients outside hospital, where it is considered necessary.

Scottish Health Advisory Service: a body set up in 1970 to prevent abuse or neglect of long-stay patients by inspecting NHS services and facilities.

Social Care Institute for Excellence: scheduled to be set up by the government in summer 2001 to review research and practice and create a knowledge base of what works in social care.

Social Services Inspectorate: part of the Department of Health that assists local government, voluntary and private bodies in the planning and delivery of social care services. It runs a national inspection programme.

Special hospitals: high-security hospitals that cater for patients with mental illness, personality disorders or learning disabilities, or often a combination of the three. These patients' behaviour can be very dangerous and many have committed serious offences. The hospitals have a dual role, combining security and therapy.

Voluntary admissions: admissions into NHS and private mental health facilities where patients have agreed to treatment without being legally compelled to.

**Other titles in the *HSJ Guide to...* range include:**

*HSJ Guide to what's happening in the NHS* priced £10.99

*HSJ Guide to what's happening in Primary Care* priced £10.99

To order your copy, ring **01483-303017**